MEDITERRANEO EDITIONS

THE FORTEZZA
THE FORTRESS OF RETHYMNO

Text
STELLA KALOGERAKI
Archaeologist

Photographs
GEORGE MARKOULAKIS

Layout
VANGELIS PAPIOMYTOGLOU

Translation into English
STELLA TSILEDAKI

Maps
VANGELIS PAPIOMYTOGLOU

Language Consultants
JOHN PAPIOMYTOGLOU
HARIS STRATIDAKIS

© copyright 2006
MEDITERRANEO EDITIONS
tel. +30 28310 21590, fax: +30 28310 21591
info@mediterraneo.gr
www.mediterraneo.gr

ISBN 960-86247-1-1

THE FORTEZZA

THE FORTRESS OF RETHYMNO

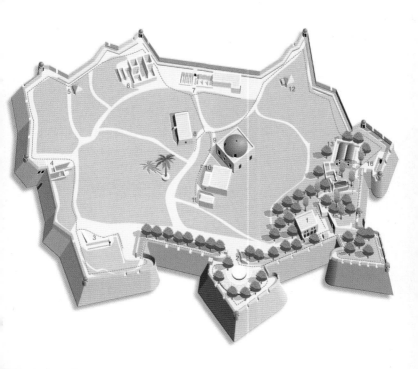

CONTENTS

RETHYMNO IN THE COURSE OF TIME

ANCIENT RITHYMNA

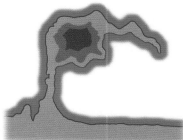

The initial form of Palaiokastro and the opposite land according to K. D. Kalokyris' theory and designs.

According to one of the first theories about Rethymno, the cape on which the town extends today was detached from the North coast, forming a kind of skerry, which was joined with the opposite side with a narrow piece of land. In the course of time the alluviums formed by the rain and the sea covered the empty space between the inslet and the land, forming the cape of Rethymno. The Neolithic sherds, which were found during surface research on the rocky hill, attest the existence of life in this phase. As the excavation of a hewn, with funeral gifts, tomb at Mastabas as well as others at Vomvoplicta and near the Cathedral, testify that there is no doubt about the existence of a settlement in the last phase of the Late Minoan period (LM III = 1350 - 1250). But the richest and most unambiguous evidences of the ancient city of Rethymno are given by the inscriptions and the coins of the 4th and 3rd centuries BC. The writers of the

The silver and bronze coins of ancient Rithymna depict the head of Athena or Apollo on one side and sea symbols, such as dolphins or trident on the other. They, also, inscribe the name of the city in various ways: PIΘY, PIΘ, PI, IP.

5

2nd and 3rd century AD give us precious information about Rithymna. **Plinius** (1st century AD) and **Claudius Ptolemeus** (2nd century AC) mentioned that it was between Pantomatrion (Panormo) and Amphimalla (Georgoupolis), while **Claudius Aelianus** (3rd century AD)mentions for the first time the existence of a sanctuary dedicated to **Artemis Roccaea**. Although there are no traces of the sanctuary, the additional information given by **H. Belli**, according to which in 1586 he visited Rethymno and pin-pointed at the Acropolis of the city pillars and relics of an ancient temple, confirms that the sanctuary of Artemis Roccaea, that Claudius Aelianus mentions, existed on the hill where Fortezza lies today. The carvings which were noticed on the natural rock inside and outside the fortress, compose another evidence for the existence of the Sanctuary on the hill. There is no doubt that during the erection of the Venetian fortress, some of the buildings and the constructions, which composed the Sanctuary, were demolished, while others were possibly covered by the landfills which were created by the construction of the bastions.

Besides, the Venetian characterization of the hill as **"Palaiokastro"** (= old castle) proves that there was fortified space with remains of the past. It is completely uncertain where exactly the settlement of ancient Rithymna was. However, some Venetians witnesses concerning the discovery of antiquities during the works at the harbour, in combination with the mosaic of roman times which was discovered during the foundation of the custom-house, and the structure with podium and pillar of the roman time too, which was discovered at the end of Arkadiou street, lead to the conclusion that the settlement during the Hellenistic and Roman period extended where Rethymno lies today. It is possible that the same happened to the settlement of ancient Rithymna, whose name has been kept alive up to now.

THE BYZANTINES, THE ARABS AND THE VENETIANS

Our information about Rethymno during the first (A') Byzantine period (325 - 824) and the period of Arab conquest (824 - 961) is not adequate. The only evidence of the Arabs presence in Rethymno is eight bronze coins found in the village of Gianoudi and kept in the Archaeological Museum of the town.The liberation of Crete by **Nikiforos Fokas** in 961 and its accession once again into the Byzantine empire means the beginning of the Second Byzantine Period, which lasted till the Venetians came to the island

6

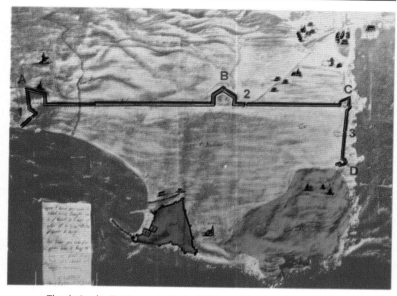

*The design by **Z. Magagnatto** in 1559 provides the only depiction of **Castrum Rethemi** and, as it can be seen, it was built next to the harbour to the East of the hill of **Palaiokastro**. This wall with the rectangular towers and two gates has not survived.*

in 1204. According to the tradition, during the second Byzantine period, 12 Byzantine families of nobles settled up in the small and unimportant settlement of Rethymno, in order to boost it. The residences were surrounded by wall, and **Castrum Rethemi** was the first form of the fortified settlement which is later mentioned as **Castel Vecchio** by the Venetians in their documents and designs.

The period of the Venetian domination typically starts in 1204 when Boniface of Monferrat had taken the lead of Crete during the fourth Crusade. Later he ceded the island to the Venetians. But soon, in 1206 the Genoese pirate **Eric Pescatore** seized the island and Venice virtually succeeded in taking it back in 1210. The distribution of the land to the Venetian settlers, the seizing of church and

The red line shows the positions where the wall of Castel Vecchio would have been built according to the plan by Magagnatto.

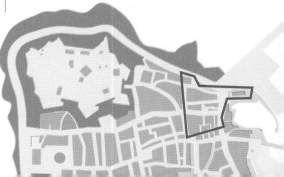

monastery lands, the injustice and the pressure exercised on the Cretans by the new conquerors, led them to react by revolting from 1211 to 1367. Regardless of the reactions, the Venetians were the masters of the island and after they had settled on Crete they began to put into practice administrative changes based on the division system of the city of Venice. Initially the island was divided into six parts and later, in the 14th century, into four, the capitals of which were Chania, Rethymnon, Candia and Sitia. The ruler of the whole island was the **Duke** (Duca) whose seat was in Candia. Every province (Chania, Rethymno, Sitia) had its own **Rettore** who governed with the help of the two **Councillors** (Consiglieri). From the first half of the 15th century the centre of **territorio di rettimo** did develop into the seat of the Latin archbishop.

So the administrative reorganization of the island benefited Rethymno, which developed into one of the major urban centers of the island with rich financial and political activity.

The division of Crete during the Venetical rule in the 14th century. Almost the same is still in force.

FROM THE DESTRUCTION OF 1571 TO THE RETHYMNO RENAISSANCE

After the conquest of Costantinople in 1453, the Venetians position in the Levant began to totter. During the 3rd Venetian-Turkish war (1537-1540) Venice lost Nauplio, Monemvasia and most of the Aegean islands. But they managed to keep Tinos, Cyprus, six of the Ionian islands and Crete to the organization of military defence with which they began to deal more.

The Veronese architect **Michele Sanmicheli** was entrusted with a programme of

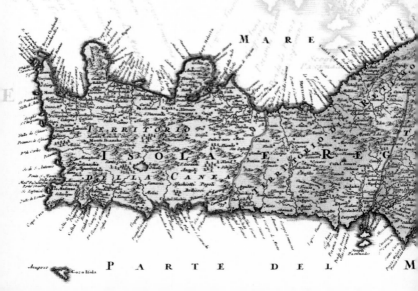

Khair ed Din Barbarossa *sacked Apokoronas, the surroundings of Chania, Rethymno and Sitia.*

fortifications which had already been arranged in 1537/38. Among his plans was the plan of the town wall, which was founded in 1540 and completed in 1570. Apart from the "official" wars, the Venetians had to fight against the pirates who controlled the Aegean sea Especially destructive were **Khair ed Din Barbarossa'** s raids in 1538, his successor's **Dragout Reis** in 1540 and **Uluz Ali** in 1571.

The last raid on 7 July 1571 was the most destructive. It was the day when the whole island was celebrating "Corpus Christi". The town was almost empty. The Venetian lords were at the surronding villages, so the population of the town seized the opportunity and avenged themselves on their Venetian Lords for the oppression and the unjustice they had sufferd at their hands by looting the town. Thus the Turkish army with Uluz Ali entered the city and finding nothing left to loot, set fire to it. Most of the houses were burnt, the walls of the Castel Vecchio and the town wall, which had just been completed, disappeared. After the total destruction, the decision for the construction of a fortress on the Palaiokastro hill, was made. According to their plans, the houses would be built in the fortress.

Indeed, in 1573, when Rettore was **Alvise Lando**, the fortress was founded. The initial plans were made by architect **Sforza Pallavicini**, and responisble for the supervision was the engineer **Gian Paolo Ferrari**. But as the materialization of the construction would delay and the

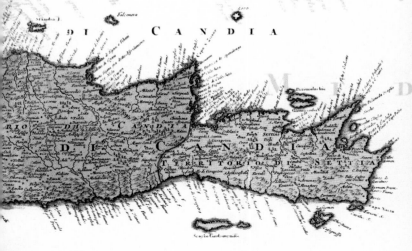

A pirate galley of Barbaria

surrounding wall, it was ascertained that the available area was too limited to enclose all the residences. So, they decided that the fortress would "offer hospitality" to the venetian administration, the Archbishop and the military authorities on permanent base and would be used as refuge of the inhabitants in case of need. Due to the levelling of the

population looked forward to it, they began to rebuild their houses in the old city, using building materials from the town wall. They, also, built their houses near it. Besides after the materialization of the

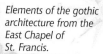

Elements of the gothic architecture from the East Chapel of St. Francis.

the architecture of the town, which adorned the buildings, disappeared. The main features of them were the double pointed arches, the cables (rope-shapped ornaments), the identations and the leafages. From now on, during the third quarter of the 16th century, the character of the town becomes renaissance, on the pattern of Venice. During this period the erection of luxurious public and private buildings took place and the town, like Venice, has a central square (**piazza**), nobbles club (**Loggia**), fountains such as the **Rimondi** fountain, a big **solar clock**, central street

and small by-passes which led to the temples, the monasteries, the mansions and other houses. Most of these splendid buildings with various door-frames, which were sometimes simple and other

The Loggia.
A design by G. Gerola

exceptionally monumental with pilasters, pillars and elaborate entablatures, representative of all renaissance architectural orders (Doric, Ionian and Corinthian), still exist witnesses of the splendid phase of the Rethymno history.

The Solar Clock.
A design by G. Gerola.

buildings caused by the destruction of 1571 and the frequent earthquakes, the gothic elements of

Rethymno and its surroundings. Depiction on parchment by F. Basilicata, 1618 (Venice, Museo Civico Correr).

Renaissance happenings at the Rimondi Fountain

11

Rethymno, Ercolo Nanni (1613)

Characteristic door-frames of Rethymno

In this renaissance environment, were the Greek element exceeded, emerged the connection of two cultures, the result of which was of special interest in the spiritual and cultural field. Scholars, such as **Marcos Musouros**, **Zaharias Kalliergis**, **Nicholaos Vlastos** and **Angelos Vergikios**, excelled in Europe, while **Georgios Hortatsis**, **Troilos** and the poet of the "Cretan War" **Marinos Tzane Bounialis**, contributed to the prosperity of native literature. The "Renaissance" in painting, where the byzantine tradition continued to play an important part, was expressed by artists such as **Emanuel Lambardos** and **Emanuel Bounialis**, who were capable representatives of the so-called "Cretan School".

*A page from "Mega Etymologikon" of **Zaharias Kalliergis**. Kalliergis was an offspring of a Byzantine family and was born in Rethymno in 1473. He is the most important Greek typographer and at the same time designer and editor of his publications. The printing office, which he founded in Venice in 1499 with Nicholaos Vlasos, was one of the most important of that time.*

Nicholaos Vlastos' *logotype. He was sponsor of Kalliergis' publications.*

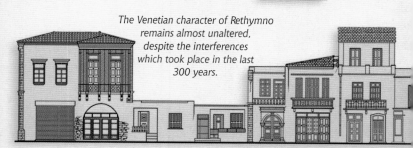

The Venetian character of Rethymno remains almost unaltered, despite the interferences which took place in the last 300 years.

*Miniature by **Angelos Vergikios**. "Kynigetika" by Oppianos. Paris, National Library. Caligrapher Angelos Vergikios worked in the reproduction laboratory in Fontainebleau and his works were for the Royal Library.*

"Madre della Consolazione", **Emanuel Tzanes** (1651). Platyteras Monastery, Corfu. Emanuel Tzanes Bounialis, brother of the "Cretan War" poet Marinos Tzanes Bounialis, was born in Rethymno in 1610 and died in Venice in 1690. His 135 known works show that sometimes he is influenced by the Byzantine patterns of the 14th and 15th century and sometimes by the West works of early Renaissance.

Georgios Hortatsis, dedicator. The church of Santa Paraskevi, Asomatoi, Rethymno.

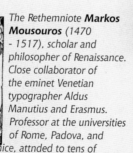

The Rethemniote **Markos Mousouros** (1470 - 1517), scholar and philosopher of Renaissance. Close collaborator of the eminet Venetian typographer Aldus Manutius and Erasmus. Professor at the universities of Rome, Padova, and Venice, attnded to tens of publications. His epigram in "Mega Etymologikon" of Kalliergis, which praises the ability of the Cretans, is characteristic.

*Our Lady "Glycophilousa", a work by **Emanuel Lambardos** (1609), Benaki Museum. In his works, which can be seen in Athens, Corfu, Sina, Jerusalem, Russia, the return to the palaeologeian and the early Cretan patterns, is obvious.*

FROM THE VENETIANS TO THE TURKS THE SIEGE OF RETHYMNO

Engraving that depicts the siege of "Thodorou", out of Chania. The inslet of "Agioi Theodoroi" was the first Cretan area that was taken by the Turks.

the disturbance of the balance was the attack against the pilgrims from Turky near Rhodes in 1644. It was obvious that a great war was about to break out. In 1645 the first Turkish troops landed in Chania and the siege started immediately. The town surrendered two months later. The great Venetian Turkish war of the 17th century had already started. On 29 September 1646, Huseyin Pasas' troops arrived before the walls of the town. But the town was weakened because of the frequent raids

The peace that Venice had succeeded in making from 1573, so as to keep the dominations in the East, was flustered by the Christian pirates' raids, especially those of the Johannite Knights in the middle of the 17th century. Katalytic to

On this depiction of the town of Rethymno in the 17th century (London, British Museum), appart from the fortress, the buildings, the town and the harbour, we can destinguish the galleys which bombarded the troops that were on the coast.

A cannon from the fortress of Rethymnon

made by the Turks, who had already settled in Chania. At the same time the soldiers' inefficiency to defend the fortress, the lack of collaboration and co-ordination with the peasants of the province of Rethymno the plague which had broken out and the inability of the Venetian fleet to help because of the rough sea, made Rethymno especially impotent to face such a well-prepared enemy. Although the situation was hopeless, when the Turks began to attack furiously and bombard the town's walls the Venetians did not lose their courage.

During the great assault against the Santa Barbara bastion, they installed two cannons at the fortress and until the end they fought by all means, in order to prevent the enemy from approaching.

The civilians had gatherd in the fortress, where the situation was dramatic, because of the plague, the wounded, the lack of food and munitions. When military Commader Minotto realised their inability for further defence, raised the white flag and negotiated under favourable condtions the surrender of Rethymnon. That is, the inhabitants, who wanted, moved to Candia, while the others became vassals of the Sultan. The fortress of Rethymno surrendered on 13 November 1646.

Venetian galley. *The disagreements among the Venetian officials about the strategy as well as the rough sea led the Venetian fleet to relative inactivity during the Turks' siege.*

RETTIMO.

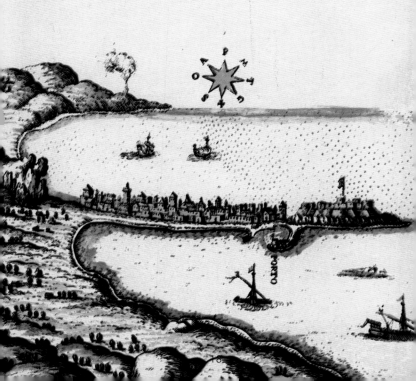

THE CHRONICLE OF THE RETHYMNON FORTIFICATIONS

In the early 14th century, when the Venetians settled in Rethymno, they found the **Castel Vecchio**, which they kept with few changes and additions until the end of 1540. As we can conclude from the Venetian documents, in the early 14th century the settlement of Rethymno, which had started to expand out of the Antico Castello walls, must have been protected by a kind of fortification

*On this map of the 15th century (Athens, Gennadeios Library) which faithfully reproduces **Chr. Buondelmondi**'s map of 1420, in the area of Rethymno apart from the peninsula with the Castel Vecchio the limits of the settlement are marked too. They are marked with a line on which part of the fortification surrounding wall, which would surround the whole suburb (burgo), is depicted.*

surrounding wall. The older but clear information we have about it, is the depiction of Rethymno on a map of Crete by Christoforo

Buondelmondi, which dates back to 1420 and we can say that it is the first topographic plan of the town.

*On the map of Crete from the Isolario by **Benedetto Bordone** whose first publication took place in 1528 in Venice, the fortified town of Rethymno is marked with the name **rettimo**. It is obvious that until the early 16th century the fortifications of Rethymnon were intact.*

◄ *Rethymnon from the East. **Marco Boschini** (1651)*

1540 - 1646

The town wall

The initial plans of the new surrounding wall of the town, which was founded in 1540, were made by the Veronese architect **Michele Sanmicheli** who was living in Rethymno from 1538 to 1540. The aim of the consruction was to surround the whole settlement to the South and would extend from sea to sea. However, the complexity of the plans on the one hand and the lack of money on the other, prevented the completion of the construction, which continued at a very slow pace and until 1560 it was not completed. It incurred the displeasure of the inhabitants who demanded the simplification of the construction so as to be quickly completed, while at the same time already from 1555 the need for the construction of the

On **Z. Magagniatto**'s map of 1559 the fortification surrounding wall has been depicted for the first time. In the East it starts from the sandy beach (sabbionara) forming the **Sta Barbara bastion (A)** in the East of which there was the **"Ammos Gate" (1)**, the bastion of **Sta Veneranda (B)** follows with a gate to the East **(2)**, and ends in the **Calergi bastion (C)**, were it turns to the North and running the rocky coast ends in another bastion (D). Between the Calergi bastion (C) and the last small bastion **(D)**, there is another gate which is called **"Squero Gate" (3)**. It is obvious that up to that moment nothing had been constructed on the rocky hill of Palaiokastro.

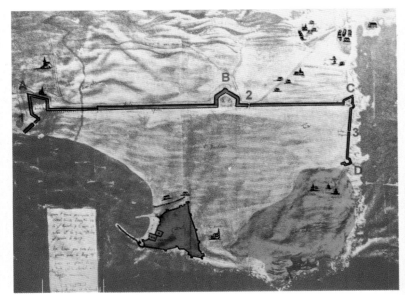

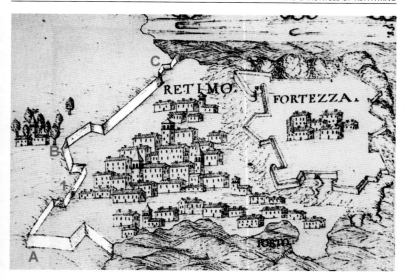

Angelo Oddi's design of 1584 is the only known, which depicts Rethymno after the destruction of 1571. Apart from the fortress which had already been built before the design was made, we can see the fortification surrounding wall of the town with the bastions of **Sta Barbara (A)**, **Sta Veneranda (B)** and **Calergi (C)**, as well as the **Guora Gate (1)**, which is correctly depicted here (that is in the East of the Sta Veneranda bastion). The part of the wall along the West rocky coast is not depicted. Generally it is not certain at all if the design gives the real picture of the town at that time, as it is known that the town wall after 1571 was abandoned and residences were built on it.

fortification on the hill of Palaiokastro was considered to be vital. So there would be free space which would be used as a shelter in case of need. The inabitants' impatience for the completion of the fortification surrounding wall was so intense that they offered money for it. The Venetian officialis on Crete suggested with formal documents the construction of the fortress on the rocky hill of Palaiokastro, because it was obvious that the defensive works were not enough as the town remained exposed and unprotected. Unfortunately the suggestions were not taken into consideration by the Venetian Senate and the total destruction came in 1571. Uluz Ali distroyed not only the walls of Castel Vecchio but also the town wall which would have been completed in 1570. The older depiction of the new fortification surrounding wall is on Zuanne Magagniatto's plan in 1559, and it must show not the initial design by Michele Sanmicheli but the alterations brought about by the Commader of Candia **Natale da Crema**. So the constructin could be

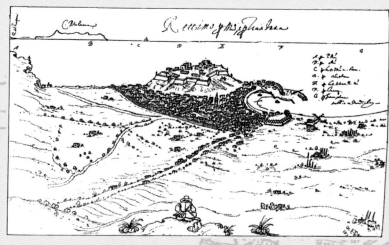

The drawing by an anonymous "painter" in 1629 (Venice, Archivio di Stato) depicts unambiguously the erection of residences on the fortification surrounding wall.

continued quickly and effectively. Despite the fact that the island's fortifications, which were planned by the great architect Sanmicheli, were faithfully completed, in Rethymno, because of the financial difficulties, his suggestions were not adopted and only the bastion of Sta Barbara was completed according to his plans.

This may be the explanation for the weakness and the incapacity of the new wall which just after its completion in 1571 and during the raid of Uluz Ali, collapsed, living the town unprotected. Then the wall was abandoned and to some degree, it was used as the base of the new residences.

We find out from a report of **Anibale Gonzaga** in 1599 that the wall of the town was almost destroyed. Althought it has nothing to do with the defensive role of the fortification surrounding wall, we have to mention the decision made in 1609 about the construction of the billets of the stradioti at the bastion of Sta Barbara. Gradually by 1640, twenty eight such billets had been built. They virtually dealt with the wall just before the Turks besieged Rethymno in 1646, when some repairs were made and a few houses were demolished, so it could be used by the soldiers.

The Fortezza

The destruction of 1571 was the motive for the erection of the fortress on the hill of Palaiokastro, which was the most appropriate position, as it was naturally fortified and from there the town, the neighboring coasts and the sea could be "overseen". Indeed, two years later, on 13 September 1573 Rettore **Alvise Lando** founded the fortress which would have been constructed according to the plans made by **Sforza Pallavicini**. The plans of Pallavicini have not been preserved, but according to the information of the manuscripts it is ascertained that Pallavicini planned a fortress of polygonal shape with two bastions on the South side (that of Sta Maria at SE corner and St Luke at the SW corner), a salient between them (St Ilias), a bastion in the middle of the East side (St Sozon), a salient (St Salvatore) at the NE corner, a salient on the North side (Sta Justine) and a salient in the West (Sto Spirito). In charge of the materialization of the structure was the engineer **Gian Paolo Ferrari**, who planned again the fortress including the alterations of Pallavicini's plan in 1574. A succession of modifications which were made, caused the inhabitants' displeasure as the completion of the destruction was behind schedule. The displeasure was intensified by the suggestion of the construction of a "spianada", that is an open area in the North of the foot of the hill Palaiokastro.

*A design by **P. Ferrari** in 1574 (Venice, Archivio di Stato) is the oldest extant plan of the fortress. The perimetric wall with the bastions at the position planned by Pallavicini, is depicted. The modification of the initial design is marked on the SE side, where the abolition of the bastion is suggestion.*

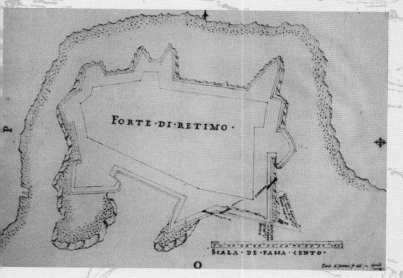

23

M.
FVRCOCH
FALO

S.ᵗᵃ MARIA
convento diftorado

S.ᵗᵒ ATANASIO
alla mare

S.ᵗᵒ Atanasio
alla spese

PORTA

SANA

PIAZZA

S. PIANATA

C

B
B
A
R
A
N
N
N
K
D
K
O
F
F
F
L
i
H
M
G
P

But it entailed the demolition of a lot of residences. Despite the disagreements, the construction proceeded as a document of 1575 informs us. In this document the detailed description of the way in which the perimetric wall was constructed as well as the first information about the organization of the buildings in the interior of the fortress are given: the Rettore's Palazzo Publico would lie in the West of the central square, near it the clock tower and the campanile of the Cathedral, in the North of the Cathedral the residence of the Archbishop and opposite it the Loggia.Commander **Manoli Mormori**, who was appointed in Rethymno approximately in 1576 and remained at least until 1582, was instrumental in the further progress in the completion of the construction. In 1578 the surrounding wall, whose length was about 1307m, had finally been completed and the time had come to build the public buildings, so the Rethemniotes would be convinced that they should start moving to the hill, according to the initial thought that the fortress would have included their residences. But the attempt did not succeed, as the population of the town had changed their mind because of the financial difficulties and the delay of the completion of the structure.

They preferred to have their houses, which had been destroyed in 1571 due to the major earthquake, repaired and live in the old town. In 1580 Rettore **Bernardo Pollani** informs with documents the Venetian Senate that 54 billets, the mlitary Commander's residence and 3 cisterns were built. The Rettore's residence was founded too. We can't have accurate information about the situation of the buildings as no contemporary plans have been preserved. In 1583 **Anzolo Barocci**, who was appointed as a Rettore, gives us information about the Rettore's residence which had been completed. It measured 33,06m X 22,62m and was a very tall construction with a particularly complicated ground floor, a lot of yards, entrances and galleries.Barocci did inaugurate the magnificent new building. We learn from Mormori's report at the end of his command in 1583 that the landfills and the parapetti had not been completed yet. However, 66 billets, the Commander's residence, the guardrooms,

◀ *About the condition prevailing within the fortress during the 17th century and before the Turkish siege the information is given mainly by maps and designs of that time. Fr. Basilicata's design of 1618 (Venice, Museo Civico Correr) is the first that gives the additional information about the position of the Commander's residence as well as the Councillors' residence next to the barracks.*

the ammunition dump, 3 cisterns and the Rettore's residence had been constructed. In 1585 **Benetto Bembo** was appointed as Rettore whose correspondence gives us the information that the fortress was still lacking in many things. The situation remained the same until 1587, when the cannon ports were completed, the parapets (parapetti) and the landfills proceeded, the storerooms, two cisterns, a powder magazine and an ammunition dump, were constructed. During his term of office, Rettore **Nicolo di Priuli** who was appointed in 1588, as well as his successor's **Luca Falier** from 1591 -1593, most construction were completed. It is ascertained by the fortress map of the Atlanda by Mormori, which dates back to that time, that is the late 16th century.

*On the drawing of Rethymno by **Mormori's Atlanda** in the 16th century (Venice, Archivio di Stato) it is obvious that the works on the hill of Palaiokastro were completed. Apart from the surrounding wall, we can distinguish the buildings in the fortress:*

Palazzo Publico
The Councillors' residence
The storerooms of the North wall
The Cathedral
The billets

The powder-magazine

PORTO.

FROM 1646 TO THE EARLY 20TH CENTURY

In 1646 starts the period of the Turkish occupation during which no significant alterations were made to the Venetian fortifications. Apart from some additions and alterations the Turks made, so as to make their presence felt in the town, generally they didn't pay any attention to the preservation of the fortifications, which soon gave a picture of decline and abandonment. Apart from the well-known small fort which they built in front of the East gate of the fortress (the today's Archaeological Museum) for its cover, all the other evidences for the fortifications are indefinite.

A precious guide to the picture of Rethymno is still the drawings and the maps of that time. Although the designs made in the second half of the 17th century do not depict accurately the town of that time, but the town as it used to be during the last years of Venetian rule. The Turkish interventions with the mosques, the minarets and the pavilions (sachnisia) are going to be described on the plans of the 18th century.

The information that is given in the

*This map by **Olfert Dapper** of 1688, clarifies that even in the late 17th century, the Turks did not make any modifications to the Venetian fortifications. The fortification surrounding wall of the town as well as the buildings in the fortress remain the same.*

◀ *During the first years of the Turkish occupation it is obvious that nothing could affect the Venetian character of the town, as we can see on the map by Marco Boschini (1651).*

monumental work by **Giuseppe Gerola**, "Monumenti Veneti nell' Isola di Creta", about the conditions prevailing in town in the early 20th century, is precious. When Gerola visited Rethymno, the construction of the new town had already started, but fortunately, a lot of parts of the Venetian fortifications as they were formed after the Turkish interventions, were still preserved.

*The French traveller **J. Pitton Tournefort**, with this drawing of 1700, gives precious information on the modification brought about by the Turks in the town of Rethymno and on the hill of the fortress: the town is full of minarets, the fortification surrounding wall can not be spotted at all and in the fortress, istead of the Cathedral, a mosque with a minaret were built.*

*On the topographical map by the English Navy Officer **G. Wilkinson**, which was designed in 1850, the complete picture of Rethymno as it was in the middle of the 18th century, is given. The blocks in the fortress, which are particularly interesting, show that the hill was being inhabited diring the Turkish domination and the pentagonal fort, which was built by the Turks to the East of the main gate of the fortress, to protect it. They, also, show the addition made to the East part of the fortification surrounding wall.*

*The "Guora" gate in a photograph by **G. Gerola***

31

THE FORTRESS DURING MODERN TIMES

Althought the Venetians did not convince the Rethemniotes to inhabit the fortress, the Turks a place of imprisonment and execution of the patriots. The Germans did install a big cannon in the pit of St Nicholas bastion, which "oversaw" supervised Rethymno from the sea side. After that period the 60's the State offered houses (out of the town) to the poor, who inhabited the fortress, and demolished the hovels in it. During the next years the process of preservation and restoration began. The study by the great Greek architect

As we can see in Behaeddin's photo (1905), in the early 20th century the Turk-Cretans built a whole town in the area of the fortress.

built a great deal of residences within the walls. After the Turks had left Rethymno, the poor of the town gradually moved to the hill and used the empty houses. the fortress was inhabited by paupers and prostitutes. The presence of prostitutes in Himarra street ended in the downgrading of the area. In Pikionis was very significant, although it did not materialize. The study of the Dr. architect I. Steriotou remains extremelyremarkable too. In the context

German soldiers "supervise" the town from the Fortezza.

of the development of the place, the Theatre "Erofili" was created in the St Ilias bastion, where from 1986 on, every summer the main performances and concerts of the well-known **Renaissance Festival** of Rethymno take place.

The "Erofili" theatre

One of the posters of the Rethymno "Renaissance Festival"

Concert in the Sultan Ibrahim mosque, in the context of the "Renaissance Festival".

THE BASICS PRINCIPLES OF THE FORTRESS ARCHITECTURE

THE BASTION SYSTEM

The institution of the cannons in the first half of the 16th century brought about the development of the fortifications, as they should be the lower polygonal constructions with the incline against the exterior wall and the basic architectural feature, which is the placing of the bastion to the corners of the polygon (fronte bastionato) was completed. According to ideal planning, the regolare). If there were differentiations among the dimensions of the parts, the fortification would be deficient (irregolare). Even the bastion, whose aim was to enter the line of the enemy so as to control a larger area and to secure the defence of the

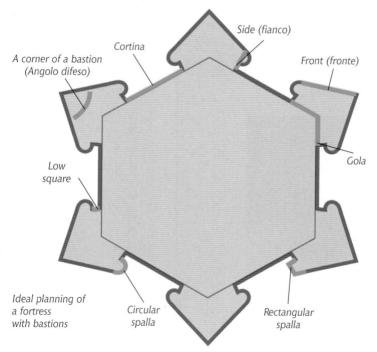

Side (fianco)

Cortina

A corner of a bastion (Angolo difeso)

Front (fronte)

Gola

Low square

Ideal planning of a fortress with bastions

Circular spalla

Rectangular spalla

equal to the new war means. So until the end of the 16th century the transition from the tall medieval fortress to polygonal fort should have equal sides and corners, so the fortification would be "regular" (fortificatione adjoining parts, was "complete", when it was pentagonal. Of course factors, such as the morphology of the terrain, the technical means and the financial situation, played their part to the construction of the "regular" and "complete" bastion. According to the descriptions of the engineers of that time a "regular" flanks (fianchi), two spalle, a low square on each side (piazze basse), a high square on each side (piazze alte), the main square (piazza del baluardo), the gola and the passages that lead to the lower squares. The principles, such as the distance between the two bastions which should not be neither particularly long nor too close, the length of the fronts in combination with the length of the cortina (= a part between two bastions) and

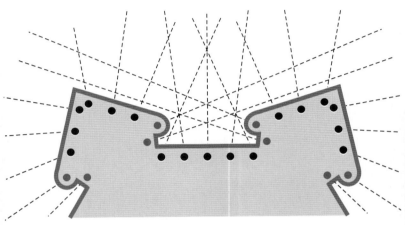

The scattering and the crossing of the shooting between two "regular" bastions (baluardo reale). As we can see, the cannons which are installed in each low square "oversee" the opposite bastion.

bastion (baluardo reale) consists of the following parts: two fronts (faccie or fronti), the corner of the bastion, two effectiveness of the defensive system with bastions depended on the extend of the application of the fundamental the form of the fortification which should incline to the circular shape.

Frankokastello *on the South side of the prefecture of Chania.*
A typical example of the medieval fortress with towers and vertical walls.

FORTEZZA
THE WALLS AND
THE BUILDINGS

THE WALLS

The enclosure wall of the Fortetza, which was built by the Venetians in the North of the town on the hill of Palaiokastro, is preserved almost intact and its initial planning has not changed. Its length is one on the North (St Nicholaos), which are the main positions of defence and the straight walls which join the bastions (cortine). Along the North and West sides, the fortification follows the rise and the fall of the rocky ground, so there are not any bastions but there the "supervision" of the coast and the in between North cortina and the North auxiliary gate. Apart from the general planning of the fortress, which is "irregular" the bastions are deficient too. They are characterized as "semi-bastions" as they have two fronts

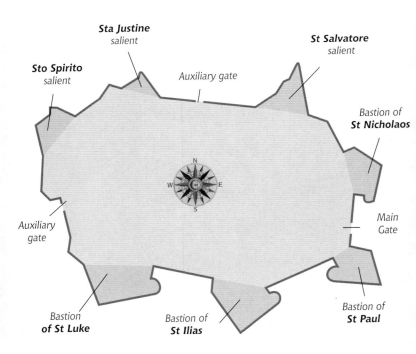

The bastions and the salients of the Fortezza were formed according to the morphology of the terrain, so the fortification is "irregular" (fortificazion irregolare).

1307m and includes four bastions: three on the South side (St Paul or Sta Maria, St Ilias and St Luke) and is a simple wall with three salients (Sto Spirito, Sta Justine and St Salvatore). The salients secured and a corner which is different for each bastion. The sides are deficient too. We can mention

The bastion of St Paul

as an example the bastion of St Luke where there is not a second side. While the four bastions have only one flank which consists of the "orecchione" (spalla with circular end) and a small straight wall which joins the orecchione with the cortina. The small wall corresponds to the "low square" where the cannons, which secured the basic defence of the fortress, were installed.

The bastion of St Nicholaos

The surrounding wall, whose maximum thickness is 1,74m, supports the landfills. It was built with rectangular stones while the interior consists of simple stonework. From bottom to top it consists of the following parts: **scarpa, cordone, parapetto**. The scarpa takes up the biggest part of the height of the wall and extends to the ground of the interior of the fortress. It is, also, inclined to support the landfills and deflect the missiles of the cannons. The cordone, which consists of a series of stones with semi-circular end, had a decorative character and at the same time prevented the climb over the walls. Finally, the parapetto is the part of the wall above the cordone in which the cannon ports and the loopholes are formed and at

Parapetto

Cordone

Scarpa

The three parts of which the external wall of the Fortezza consists.

The parapetto over the main gate of the Fortezza

40

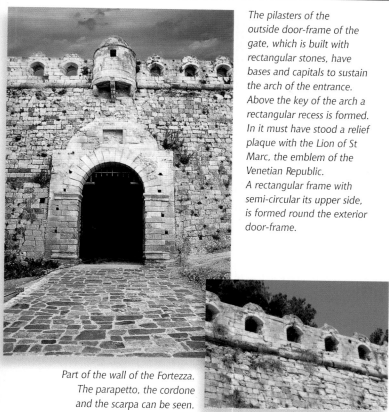

The pilasters of the outside door-frame of the gate, which is built with rectangular stones, have bases and capitals to sustain the arch of the entrance. Above the key of the arch a rectangular recess is formed. In it must have stood a relief plaque with the Lion of St Marc, the emblem of the Venetian Republic.
A rectangular frame with semi-circular its upper side, is formed round the exterior door-frame.

Part of the wall of the Fortezza. The parapetto, the cordone and the scarpa can be seen.

the same time it secured the cover of the soldiers. Behind the parapetto in the North of the surrounding wall there is a kind of elevated passage (banchetta) for the transport of the soldiers behind the wall. In the East of the surrounding wall, and between the two bastions (St Pauls' and St Nicholaos') stands the **Main Gate** of the Fortress, the position of which was wisely chosen as from the East the fortress ran little danger of being attacked and the approach to it from the town was direct. The two bastions in the North and the South secured its cover, while in the East it

The Sta Justine salient

was substantially uncovered since the pentagonal fort, which was in front of the entrance (the today Archaeological Museum) did not exist during Venetian domination as it is a Turkish addition. As a whole, the main gate consists of a gallery whose length is 26,80m.

The relief plaque with the Lion of St Marc built in the outer part of the wall, between the bastions of St Luke and St Ilias. It is proportionate to the one which would adorn the recess above the central gate.

and width 3,80m. The gallery as well as three areas to the South which are covered with semi-cylindrical vaults, have been formed in the landfills of

the wall. Apart from the main gate, the needs for supply of food and munitions in case of siege, made essential the construction

Section of the gallery of the East gate with the two arched openings through which the communication with the three guardrooms took place.

Ground plan of the gallery of the East gate with guardrooms in the North.

The entrances to the guardrooms in the North of the gate

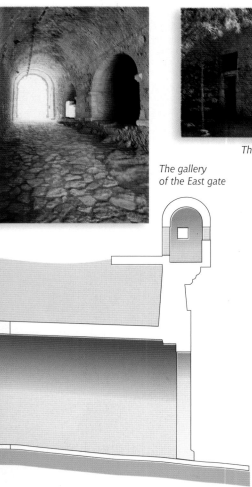

The gallery of the East gate

of other **auxiliary gate** at the suitable points of the surrounding wall. There are two auxiliary gates, one on the **West** and one on the **North** side. A path joined the north one with the coast from where the access to small boats with the help of a ladder was possible. A lot of people escaped using this path during the Turkish siege of the fortress.

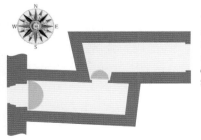

The West auxiliary gate is in the South of the Sto Spirito salient. It consists of two rectangular, parallel areas with semi-cylindrical vaulted roofs and a small opening to allow communication, leading to two large cannon ports.

The Fortezza from the West

The outer side of the West auxiliary gate with the arched lintel and the worn, built-in, relief emblem, is closed today. Once this gate allowed the entrance of the population to the fortress not only in case of need but also in peace time

The arched door-frame of communication between the two rectangular areas of the West auxiliary gate.

Two rectangular, vault-roofed, areas in the North of the West auxiliary gate, was used as cannon ports which covered it and at the same time "oversaw" the hill of Palaiokastro.

The North auxiliary gate between the salients of Sta Justine and St Salvatore, has a door-frame with an arched lintel.

The curved on the natural rock steps, which lead to the West auxiliary gate of the fortress, documents that there was a subsidiary road from West Chania running the West side of the wall, to the coast.

One of the main features of the surrounding wall of the fortress is **the guardooms** (guardiole) at the parapetto level, which were used for the stay of the soldiers, who went on patrols.

On the whole, there are ten circular guardrooms and one rectangular: over the main gate, at the bastion of St Paule, at the bastion of St Ilias (a circular and a rectangular), at the salient to the North of the West auxiliary gate, at the bastion of St Nicholaos, at the bastion of St Luke and at the salients of Sto Spirito, Sta Justine and St Salvatore.

The North guardroom of the St Nicholaos bastion. As a rule the guardrooms of the fortress consist of a circular wall with cordone above which a small vault develops. Every guardroom has three loopholes. This is one of the two which exceptionally do not have a cordone.

The guardroom of the Sta Justine salient

The guardroom over the main gate

The flag-post next to the South guardroom of the orecchione of bastion of St Nicholaos. There is a similar construction next to the guardroom of the St Luke bastion.

of the bastion. There is no room for doubt that this construction was a contramina from which started galleries running the whole underground area of the fortress. Except the "wells", other complementary constructions for the support of the defensive effectiveness of the surrounding wall, were the **cavalieri**, that is the landfills in some areas of the fortress at the

Concerning the defensive systems which are connected with the surrounding wall, we have to mention the underground

At the fortress of Rethymno, there is such a construction in the landfills of the bastion of St Ilias and its entrance is on the East supporting wall

The contramina of the bastion of St Ilias is an underground construction, which constists of a rectangular area covered with a semi-spherical arch and a passage whose length is 16,55m and width is 2,5-3m and has a direction to the South. This passage is covered with a semi-cylindrical arch, has stone parapet walls and ends in a circular area. At the centre of this circular area there is a well opening which is covered by a vault from the top of which starts a pipe which ends in an opening at the ground level of the bastion.

constructions or wells / **counter-mines** (contramini) which are formed in the landfills or at the base of the wall or out of the wall so as to confront the hostile undermining.

The entrance to the contramina in the bastion of St Ilias, as it can be seen from the stage of the theatre.

basic level of the landfills of the whole surrounding wall. Apart from of the "control" of the region, the cover of the fortress interior was secured by the landfills, which were put in the most disadvantageous first one is on bastion of St Luke and the second on the main gate. The cavaliere of this bastion was constructed for the cover of the interior of the fortress and its buildings, which were exposed to the hill of St Athanasios (to the West of the town, on the road to Chania). It consists of a construction in the shape of Γ, which supports the landfills and may be used for the stay of the soldiers on guard. The East gate cavaliere rises above the cortina and consists of the landfills of its arcade.

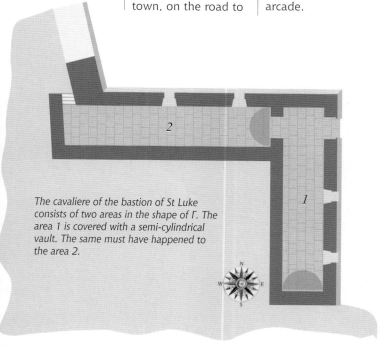

The cavaliere of the bastion of St Luke consists of two areas in the shape of Γ. The area 1 is covered with a semi-cylindrical vault. The same must have happened to the area 2.

areas which should be covered and had semi-cercular or rectangular shape. In the fortress of Rethymno there are two cavalieri. The

The East side of the area 1 of the St Luke cavaliere.

A view of the St Luke cavaliere from the North

Its aim was on the one hand the providing of better defence to the vital side of the main gate and on the other hand the cover of the interior of the fortress. In conclusion, the planning of the surrounding wall was not the best possible, as a result its defensive capacity was limited. Its "irregularity" because of the rocky ground, the lack of moat, the limited area round it, because of the inhabitants refusal to demolish their houses, as well as the fact that it was exposed to the hill of St Athanasios in the West of the town, are some of the most important reasons for its limited difensive capasity. On the contrary, the planning of the interior was ruther correct, thanks to the removal of the public buildings from the walls, the placing of the powder-magazines on the North safe side and the shaping of the square in the centre.

THE BUILDINGS

The Artillery magazine

After crossing the gallery of the main gate, the two-storeyed building we encounter on the right, is the artillery magazine whose use is documented by the annotations of the Venetian plans. According to the Venetian documents it was constructed approximately in 1581, when Bernardo Pollani was the Rettore of Rethymno. It was used for storing cannons, arming, munitions and cereals.

O. Maghazeni per l'artiglieria

Basilicata in the annotation of the map in 1618 characterizes the first building which we meet on the right when we enter by the East gate of the fortress, as "maghazeni per l' artiglieria", that is artillery magazine.

The ground floor of the artillery magazine consists of two rooms. Each one along its central axis has three pillars. These rooms, between which a wall rises, communicate through an arched opening. On the analogy of the ground floor, the upper storey consists of two rooms too. It is roofed with semi-cylindrical vaults, the upper surface of which forms a flat roof. At the extension of the West side there is an arch, on which the water pipe runs from the roof of the storeroom to the cistern that was in the bastion of St Ilias.

The South side of the artillery magazine with the four arched openings of the ground floor. On this side there are two plaques built in the wall which are very worn and may be depicted an emblem.

The Councillors' residence

The area of the Sta Justine salient was chosen by the Cretan noble F. Lambardos to build his luxurious residence which was ceded to the Venetian andministration and occupied by one of the two Councillors, as the second should be within the town, to keep track of current events and maintain the order. The use of the two-storeyed building and the construction in the West, which was used as barracks, is documented by the annotations of the Venetian plans.

In the annotation of the map of 1618 Basilicata refers to the construction in the Sta Justine salient: P=casa del conseier (the Councillors residence) and F= Quartieri (= barracks).

The groundfloor consists of a central corridor running the length of the building with two rooms opening off on each side. The arch-roofed small area between the two rooms of the West side leads to the exterior of the building.

The same arrangement was followed on the upper floor, where there is a room which was covered with a small vault and was rather used as a Turkish bath.

The Councillors' residence from the West

The Rettore's residence

In the West of the main square of the fortress, opposite the Cathedral, the construction of the Rettore's residence was built. Only a part has been preserved up to now. The building, whose construction was completed in 1582, was founded in 1575 and inaugurated by the stay of Rettore Anzolo Barocci, who continued to make alterations until 1584, as it was considered to be too tall and exposed to the hill of St Athanasios, in the West of the town. Its stateliness and luxury are testified in the documents of the time as it was mentioned to have had 49 doors, 81 windows, 2 staircases and balkonies. Unfortunately, nothing except a part of a prison which was constructed by Barrocci in the East of the main residence, has been preserved.

Basilicata, in the annotation of the map that dates back to 1618, refers to the building H as Palazzo.

The part of the Rettore's residence that has been preserved, consists of an almost rectangular area covered with a semi-cylindrical arch. On the East side there are two rectangular openings from which only the one was used as an entrance, while on the North side the circular opening was used as a skylight. In the South of this area there is a second smaller area covered with a semi-cylindrical arch, too.

The Rettore's residence from the West

The Rettore's residence from the South.

53

The Bishop's Palace (?)

The isufficient information from the Venetian documents concerning the use of the building in the South of the mosque makes difficult its identification with the Bishop's palace, a glamorous and imposing structure which had already been erected in 1575. The Venetian maps and plans do not depict a building in this area, so the identification of the two buildings becomes more difficult.

The Bishop's Palace consists of two buildings, from which one is smaller than the other. They must have been buit in different periods, as we can see from the joint of the South side which proves that the smaller building is a latter construction. The larger building is roofed with two semi-cylindrical vaults which are supported by two arches at the point of their joint in the centre of the building, as well as by two arches and three pillars on the East wall and by three arches and four pillars on the West. The entrance as well as two windows were on the North side. The smaller plain building, next to the bigger, is also, roofed with a semi-cylindrical arch and apart from the opening of the entrance on the North side has three loopholes. The utility of the small rectangular area in front of the entrance is unknown.

The Bishop's Palace from the NW.

The Cathedral Sultan Ibrahim Mosque

In the main "square" of the Fortezza, opposite the imposing residence of the Rettore the Cathedral of Rethymno was founded by Bishop

*The Venetian plans like the one of **M. Boschini** (1651), depict the Duomo with its bell tower.*

Chiapone in 1583. It was dedicated to St Nicholaos.
The need for the construction of a new Cathedral was

pressing, as the old one was detroyed during the raid of Uluz Ali in 1571. Bishop Carrara refused in 1585 to celebrate mass in the new Cathedral as the interior was not large enough but later, in 1586, Rettore Benetto Bembo solved the problem as the fullfilment of the soldiers' religious tasks was considered to be necessary. On the ruins of the Cathedral of St Nicholaos, whose position is documented by the Venetian plans, the mosque of Sultan

Ibrahim was built destroying almost every part of the Venetian building. The huge semi-spherical dome, the mihrab niche in the middle of the SE side and the minaret which rised next to the entrance, are the features that show the new muslim character of the building.

The closed pipe of the NE side of the mosque distributed the rain water from the roof to one of the cisterns which were near the North wall of the fortress.

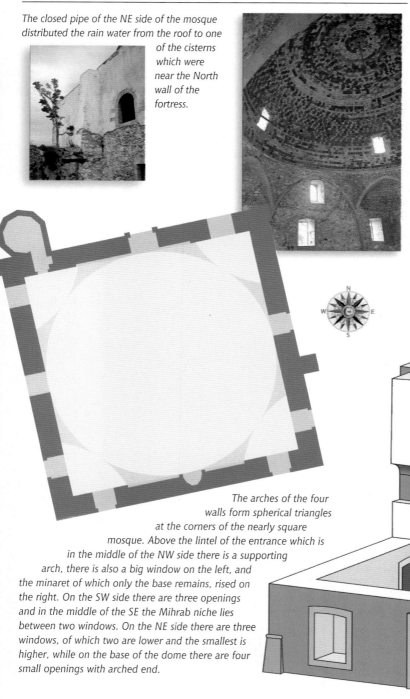

The arches of the four walls form spherical triangles at the corners of the nearly square mosque. Above the lintel of the entrance which is in the middle of the NW side there is a supporting arch, there is also a big window on the left, and the minaret of which only the base remains, rised on the right. On the SW side there are three openings and in the middle of the SE the Mihrab niche lies between two windows. On the NE side there are three windows, of which two are lower and the smallest is higher, while on the base of the dome there are four small openings with arched end.

In the middle of the SE side of the mosque, was formed the polygonal niche of mihrab whose height is 2m. Its semi-conical cover is decorated with relief "stalactite". The same pattern of "stalaktites" in combination with the leaves in the shape of heart, develops on the cornice, that in turn develops in the niche, while under the cornice there are engraved circular rosettes.

The storerooms of the North wall

The main complex of storerooms of the fortress is constructed along the North wall, between the Sta Justine and St Salvatore salients. The reasons for the erection of the building on this particular side was on the one hand the long distance from the most dangerous and easy to attack South side of the wall and on the other its proximity to the North auxiliary gate from where the fortress was supplied, as there was a path through which it communicated with the coast.

The site of the storerooms remained the same not only during Venetian rule but also during the Turkish domination, as the plans of the fortress document. The complex was founded in 1584 by Rettore Anzolo Barocci and the last modificationes were made by Rettore Nicolo di Priuli in 1591.

The layout of the storage area is the following: in the West of the corridor with the stairs and the landings, which lead to the North auxiliary gate and exactly next to it is the underground area 1 which is roofed with a semi-cylindrical arch whose length is 9 m. Opposite it, the underground area 2 is 51 m. long and roofed with a semi-cylindrical arch on which the passage, where the soldiers moved, was formed. In the South of the area 1, develops the rectangular underground area 3 that is divided in three parts by two arcades. In the East of the main corridor is formed the rectangular underground area 4, which is 14m. long and about 10m. wide, with windows and semi-pillars on the wall and in the centre two pillars which are linked by two arches. In the east of the area 4 the building 5 rises. It consists of two parts (a smaller

and a bigger), roofed with semi-cylindrical arches. We enter the building through the small area where there is a staircase that leads to the main store-house which in turn has a window in the East and two in the West. In the East of the areas 3, 4, 5, the outlets of 8 ventilators which lead to the underground area, were brought to light.

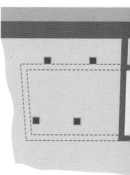

The staircase of the entrance of area (5)

The underground elongated store-room (2)

The pillars of the underground storeroom (4)

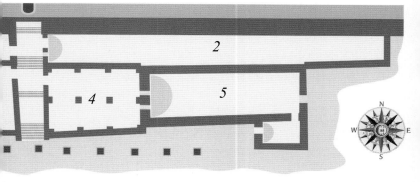

The Powder-Magazines

The prerequisite for the choice of the powder-magazines position was its distance from the first line of defence, that is the South side of the fortification surrounding wall. So they were built along the North wall, within long distance and with teir courtyards for safety. In this way the lack of powder would have been avoided, if an explosion had taken place in case of siege. There were three powder-magazines from which only two have survived up to now. The first in the Sta Justine salient (a) and the second in the St Salvatore salient (b). An explosion in 1631 destroyed the third.

The powder-magazine (a) is vault-roofed and its height is 4,60m. Its entrance is on the NW side and a ventilation opening on the NE. On the SW side there was a small, rectangular area with which it communicated.

The roofing of the powder-magazine (b) is pyramidical and its total height is 3,90m. Its entrance was on the North side of a small rectangular area whose covering has not preserved. On its North wall there is a ventilation opening.

The cisterns

Rethymno got water from the spring of S. Zuanne on the hill of Prophet Ilias in the South of the town, from where the watermain extened and ended in the Rimondi fountain, in the central square, supplying the population with water. Of course the water could not be brought up to the fortress, so cisterns were constructed in order to supply the fortress with water. The rain-water was collected on the roofs of the buildings and led off into the cisterns. The conduits, which can be seen even today in the whole area of the fortress, correspond to the cisterns among which the one of the St Ilias bastion is of special interest and served as a contramina, that is an underground defensive construction.

The building near the St. Nicholaus bastion

The documents and the plans of the time give no information regarding the use of this twin building, which must have been a storeroom or a workshop.

The South view of the building.

Around the building on the SE part of the West side, there is a courtyard whose entrance is on its South end.

The rectangular area of the building is devided in two parts which are roofed with two semi-cylindrical arches. The building has two entrances, one in the East and one in the South, two rectangular windows on each side (North, East) and two skylights, one below each arch.

The church of St Theodore

Near the bastion of St Nicholaos stands the typical domed church with a single nave that named after its dedicator Theodore de Chiostak, Russian Commander of Rethymno during the first years of the political self-rule.

The St Theodore Trichinas church, which was dedicated on 21 March 1899, was possibly constructed on an older church, as some Venetian designs document. The designs depict a small building that is similar to the church.

Although during Venetian rule the inhabitants of Rethymno refused to build their houses within the fortress and move there according to the plans of the Venetian administration, the ruinous buildings near the church of St Theodore Trichinas testify to the habitation of the fortress during the Turkish occupation and until the first half of our century.

A WALK

In the North of Rethymno, near the sea, dominates the rocky hill of Palaiokastro, in a unique and ideal position to "offer hospitality" to the Venetian fortress of the town. We can approach the Fortezza through three different ways: Himarras street, the cobbled road of

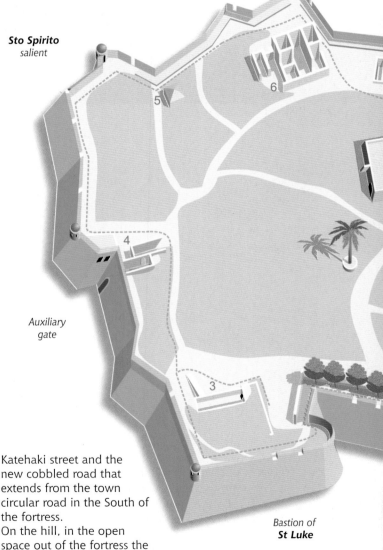

Sta Justine
salient

Sto Spirito
salient

*Auxiliary
gate*

*Bastion of
St Luke*

Katehaki street and the new cobbled road that extends from the town circular road in the South of the fortress.
On the hill, in the open space out of the fortress the pentagonal fort is situated which during the Turkish domination protected the main gate of the Fortezza and today houses the Archaeological Museum of the town.

The East gate of the fortress (p. 41) with its impressive cannonports and the guardroom at the parapetto consists of a gallery with two arched recesses in the North, which once led to three areas that functioned as guardrooms. After crossing the gallery, on the right we meet the **artillery magazine (1)** (p. 51) with four arched openings on the ground floor.

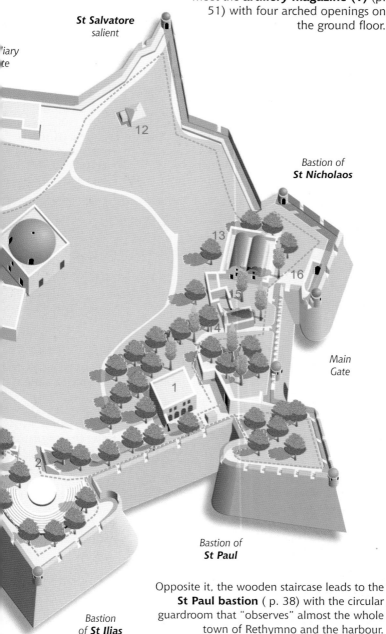

St Salvatore
salient

'iary
te

Bastion of
St Nicholaos

Main Gate

Bastion of
St Paul

Bastion of St Ilias

Opposite it, the wooden staircase leads to the **St Paul bastion** (p. 38) with the circular guardroom that "observes" almost the whole town of Rethymno and the harbour.

THE FORTEZZA - THE FORTRESS OF RETHYMNO

Walking to the West at the point where the second bastion is, we meet the openings of two "wells" that functioned as **contramina (2)** (p. 46) that is underground galleries for the confrontation of the enemy sapping. In the **St Ilias bastion** (p. 38), the "Erofili" theatre every summer, from 1986, "offers

extends from sea to sea and our look rests only on the massif that rises in the South of Rethymnon. Leaving behind the bastion of St Ilias and walking along the parapetto, we reach the bastion of **St Luke** (p. 38) with the circular guardroom on its salient. The

The "Erofili" theatre

North, we meet the area of the West auxiliary gate with **the cannon emplacement (4)** next to it (p. 43). Following the course

The St Luke cavaliere

hospitality" to the performances and concerts of the "Renaissance Festival" of Rethymnon. The cirular guardroom and the square one, which is unique in the whole fortress, offer panoramic view of the town which

homonymous cavaliere (3) (p 47), which was formed in the centre of the bastion to secure the cover of the fortress against the opposite hills, consists of two buildings in the shape of Γ, which support the landfills. Walking to the

of the wall now we are reaching first **the Sto Spirito salient** with the circular guardroom and then the one of the two **powder-magazines (5)** of the fortress (p. 60). Then in the **St Justine salient** stands the imposing two-storeyed the **Counsillors' residence (6)** (p. 52).

The Councillors' residence.